A Careful Hunger

A Careful Hunger

Poems

Judy Young

Edited by John K. Young

*Foreword by Mary Ann Taylor-Hall
and Susan Starr Richards*

Scholarly publisher for the Commonwealth,
serving Bellarmine University, Berea College, Centre
College of Kentucky, Eastern Kentucky University,
The Filson Historical Society, Georgetown College,
Kentucky Historical Society, Kentucky State University,
Morehead State University, Murray State University,
Northern Kentucky University, Transylvania University,
University of Kentucky, University of Louisville,
and Western Kentucky University.

Editorial and Sales Offices: The University Press of Kentucky
663 South Limestone Street, Lexington, Kentucky 40508-4008
www.kentuckypress.com

Cataloging-in-Publication data is available from the Library of Congress.

ISBN 978-0-8131-7784-7 (paperback : alk. paper)
ISBN 978-0-8131-7786-1 (epub)
ISBN 978-0-8131-7785-4 (pdf)

This book is printed on acid-free paper meeting
the requirements of the American National Standard
for Permanence in Paper for Printed Library Materials.

Manufactured in the United States of America

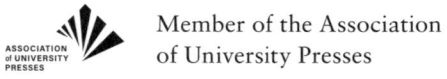

Member of the Association
of University Presses

Contents

Foreword

We never called it The Art Group. That definite article was way too definite for us. Likewise the capital letters. We called it art group, or just group. Mainly, we just said, "Can everybody meet Thursday the twenty-third? And where?"

It took a while to collect ourselves, but finally there were seven of us: Donna Boyd, our musical genius; Carolyn Hisel, an extraordinary painter of light-filled rooms, mysterious landscapes, pure souls, and comical little figures; the writer/poets Susan Richards, Mary Ann Taylor-Hall, and Jane Gentry. Audrey Robinson and Judy Young were both visual artists and poets.

Judy had been a student in a poetry workshop taught by Mary Ann's husband, James Baker Hall. He introduced Judy to Mary Ann, thinking, quite rightly, that they'd be glad to know each other. So they got accustomed to meeting for lunch every few weeks, where they may have talked a little about their lives as writers, but also, most urgently, about the organization of their clothes closets.

Then one day (no one can remember exactly the year—we're guessing 1985), Judy came out to Mary Ann's home in Harrison County, Kentucky, for lunch and brought with her Audrey Robinson. Audrey had come to Lexington with her husband, Don Robinson, from a commune in Northern California because Don needed to help his aging father run the family horse farm. She felt out of place in the horse world of Fayette County, pining for California and her lost Tassajara life. A less similar pair than Audrey and Judy could hardly be imagined, but a teacher at The Lexington School, where they both had children enrolled, had suggested that they might like to meet each other. Audrey told us, years later, about Judy wearing a suit to visit her for the first time. "A suit!" said Audrey, still shocked. "And heels!" Audrey was receiving company that day barefoot, in her usual shorts and T-shirt. But they learned quickly that the teacher who introduced them was right—they *did* have a lot in common. Both of them were writing poetry. And both were free-ranging visual artists—mainly painting for Judy and sculpting for Audrey—but both of them exploring many new art forms.

Anyway, on that afternoon in Harrison County, they told us about a group of women who were calling themselves the Stuck Artists. The group had been organized by the art photographer Linda Butler (about to decamp for Pittsburgh).

Well, both Mary Ann and Sue were, for complicated reasons, good and stuck at the time, so it sounded at least nonthreatening and worth a try. Their game, Judy and Audrey explained, was to pull three words out of a box and go home and play with them. And come back in three weeks with whatever they'd made of them.

Play became the operative word.

The idea was to let ourselves loose, and we did. We remembered how to play. We loved what we were doing. We stopped calling our group anything. We just drew the words out of a box and went home to do something with them.

We—Mary Ann and Sue—both thought of ourselves, when we entered the festivities, as unadulterated fiction writers with a certain degree of accomplishment out in the world, both a little overwhelmed by what our imaginations commanded us to create. After we joined the party, we each completed novels and short fiction, propelled and liberated by this new attitude of "Just let it fly. Just get something to bring to our next meeting." The necessity of creating something in three weeks, something brief enough to read in the group, directed us toward shorter forms—particularly poetry, which allowed us access to our immediate personal experience of being alive in rural Harrison County.

These meetings and the ritual that governed them freed all seven of us. We had fun. We were boisterous, often raucous. Once, after a meeting at Carolyn's house, her husband Alan, who'd been banished to his study in the basement, told her, "I never heard a group of people laugh so much. And so loud!" Carolyn said, "Now you understand why we don't let you guys come to our meetings." To which Alan replied, "I don't see why you ever let us come to *anything*."

So we had about thirty years of artistic bliss together—a faithful, attentive, honest audience, always eager to see what we had created, to offer help, or applaud finished works. We were excellent critics, and as a group, our variety of art forms enriched the process. Donna, our musicologist, brought insights to our poems that no strictly literary group could have produced. And the responses of the word people to the visual people, and vice versa, sometimes opened new and thrilling ways of seeing our work.

Through all those years, Judy was with us entirely. We were all recipients of her intuitive, almost mystical kindness, in one form or another. Through every sort of trouble, Judy understood what was happening. Here is one example: She and Jane got to be friends while they waited for their kids to get out of school every weekday. To pass the time in a useful way as they sat in Judy's car, they told each other what they had dreamed. One day Judy reported a strange dream she'd had, about a house she did not know. Still, she described the house in detail, upstairs and downstairs, kitchen, curtains and carpets and furniture, even its atmosphere, which was heavy with sadness and anger. "But I've never seen this house, much less been inside it," she told Jane. "I don't know where it is or whose it is."

Foreword

"I do," Jane said. She was weeping. "It's my house. You're dreaming my life." The heavy, sad, angry atmosphere of the house was also Jane's, as she endured a particularly bad time in her life. Such was Judy's generosity—of imagination, of psychic understanding. She was willing to give over her dreams to her friends. To inhabit their sadness, a feat way beyond mere sympathy.

We all understood and respected Judy as a person of many layers—a practical, poised, somewhat public person (for one who was so basically private), with an instinctive kindness, an understanding of what was needed, and a willingness to provide it. And, beneath that, some other spirit, mysterious and unreachable.

When she began writing the poems for this collection, born at least partly out of the love and freedom our group of friends offered, those new poems allowed her to reveal the terrible history of her childhood: from before the time she could remember, she'd been repeatedly raped by her father. As a result, she suffered lifelong depression, fear, and guilt. Like many survivors of early sexual abuse, she developed an eating disorder and felt compelled to eat desperately to save herself for a moment from her old fears. Her father used to walk her downstairs and fix her breakfast afterward, thus forever teaching her that food was a reliable means of escape and solace. He also terrified her into silence. Until she was well into middle age, she could not bring herself to talk about—or even think about—her childhood trauma.

"You can't heal it if you don't feel it," they say, meaning the pain that life has given you. Judy was in therapy for years, learning to admit what had happened to her at the beginning of her life. Too often, it seemed to be happening right then, in her mind and body: her father's old rage rising within her at any moment, in the form of panic and depression, driving her to rush out and buy a half-gallon of vanilla ice cream, take it home, eat it all. So that's the story: her life is early ruined, in the time when she was completely innocent and defenseless, by a man she loved and trusted, and to whom she was utterly vulnerable as the ruling authority in her life.

Yet that's not the whole story. Her life is not ruined. There is joy in this book, an almost unbearable joy.

Her life is saved—by herself, her own desperate courage and determination, by the grace and beauty she finally found for herself in her good marriage and her good kids, her orderly, welcoming house full of art, and by her truth-telling to this group of women friends who loved her and her work. Her life is saved most of all by this book, this stunning object of art she created out of her own nightmare beginnings. Because the truth is that your pain doesn't save you, not even when you can feel it. You have to keep searching for what will heal you.

Judy found it in poetry.

And she found it in the lake.

When Judy and Byron built their house on Lake Hickman, she discovered in its creatures and its waters a connection with the natural world, which she had never before felt. She especially loved the birds, who were real, live creatures, comical and beautiful, mysterious and ordinary, to be fed, studied, listened to, and learned from. They also became her familiar spirits—symbols of the soul, and at the same time, of death, as birds have always been in human story.

In the last year of her life, Judy felt death waiting for her. Jane, her best friend, was dying of cancer, and Judy kept seeing the figure of a blue woman at the edge of her vision. She was not sure if that figure was Jane or herself, but it frightened her, she told us; she thought it meant that she, too, was about to die. Sue tried to talk her out of that notion, saying blue was the color of the spirit, and it might just mean that she was finding her way back to the pure soul her father had stolen, along with her body, years before.

Maybe they were both right. The voice of the penultimate

poem in this collection, "Migration," is wild and ecstatic. If you have never heard the migratory birds calling to each other as they travel overhead on spring or fall nights, you may not understand how their cries convey the desperate excitement, exultation, and danger of traveling from one world to another.

But you can get the sense of it from this poem.

We are continually inspired by Judy's courage, by the way she fought daily to live her life, with the nightmare of her childhood still alive in her. And by the way she faced toward her death as she sensed it before her—finishing this book, putting it together, leaving it there on her desk for us and the world to read.

Mary Ann Taylor-Hall
Susan Starr Richards

A Note on the Text

Judy Young (1940–2015) did not seek to publish this book. She did collect many of the poems here under the title *A Careful Hunger,* as part of a series of manuscripts (sometimes under different titles) she produced and revised during the second half of her life. About fifteen years after her graduation from Transylvania University in 1962, Young returned to academic studies of literature and writing, first at the University of Kentucky, and then through the low-residency MFA program at Warren Wilson College, where she worked primarily with poets Joan Aleshire and Gregory Orr. She submitted earlier versions of two poems included here, "Song for Which There Are No Words" and "A Scientific Education," to the *Journal of Kentucky Studies,* where they appeared in the October 1986 issue, along with three other poems not included in this collection. It was Young's only creative publication. At various points, she established provisional collections of her best work for possible submissions to a press, but always ultimately refrained from that step, anxious about the prospect of reading often deeply personal poems in a public setting.

A Careful Hunger represents a version of the final form Young had made for her works before her death in January 2015. Sue Richards, Mary Ann Taylor-Hall, and I have edited that manuscript, selecting among variant lines where needed and restoring some early poems, to more fully convey the scope of a private literary career. We have also responded to the thoughtful and careful suggestions provided by two anonymous UPK reviewers. As an editorial practice, it seems reasonable to conclude that my mother would have revised both individual poems and the manuscript as a whole, in something like the process we have used, though she doubtless would have made different decisions about specific lines and the poems' organization than we have. Contemporary editorial theory holds editing to be an inherently interpretive practice: there is no "definite" text that an edition seeks to reflect, but an array of possible texts from which an edition chooses, or enables readers to choose themselves. Sadly, two of my mother's closest friends and I are only in the position of making such choices because she is not here to do so—or to choose not to do. Speaking for myself, I can only hope that this edition honors an always loving and thoughtful mother who taught me how to read closely and carefully, attentive to both direct and indirect textual expressions, as well as the spaces between them.

This collection traces the path of a woman finding her poetic voice in middle age: returning to an often painful childhood; using her extensive travels through Europe and Asia for stray sparks of inspiration; closely observing the natural world, especially the populations of birds moving through the space between her back porch and the lake below; and meditating on the nature of creativity. It is a life's work.

John K. Young
September 2018

Blue Kitchen with East Window

The empty
       glass on the table,

plates draining in the splattered sink,
       and all the knives lined
             so carefully

in their subtle arrangement—

             Is it madness to think of them?—

The half-heated kettle
       rattles high-
             pitched and certain:

I am alive and must say so
one way or another.

History

I want to give my history away,
those ragged years of hand-me-down

questions, the impossible days,
the exhaustion of evenings.

I want to bury the past
in the lake's decaying silt

where turtles sleep, in winter,
with rotten grass

between their teeth and bones
of ducklings in their guts.

Brightness

Awake early, I catch
the sun blinding trees,
smudging mallards,
tarnishing the lake.

Honey locusts jitter
against the window,
twitching, manic,
restless as memory.

I hunker like a question mark
over my notebook where
the frantic stupor of the past
zigzags off the page.

Fists of sunlight
strike my words,
break them open:

I do not have to return
to the beginning.

Little Girl, Little Girl

1

Little girl, little girl,
where are the fairy tales,
even the false ones

cast against the last
of the sun?
                    I enter

the darkness that exists
at the edge of light,
a mortal who ages

each second, using
someone else's air,
speaking the wrong lie.

2

Past the fields of tall grass
and Queen Anne's lace
I sleep without dreaming.

The leaves overnight
rush into color
as if some sign were given.

I content
myself with whispers
inside the skin of my life.

3

What did they talk about afterward,
as he fed her kumquats
almost bruised
to ripeness?

In the bed so small,
so used and broken.

4

She remembered that there were no trees
and the sky was insignificant.
What she spoke in darkness
could not be heard in sun.

Surely he will not harm me, she thought,
as she pushed her hands through the thick black fur
to find the path that leads
into the heart of the world.

Secrets

How safe can it be to sleep?
Lie still. Don't breathe. Play dead.

I am the one I can't see.
I hear her breathing,
dream her dreams in the dark room

inside me.

Who am I?
Or did I die in some other fairy tale?
Who will cut open the belly and set me free?

I see the slit and the wet jewels spilling out.

Music

Starch splatters my mother's arms
as she glides a shirt through the wringer.
Her fingers glisten and the music
in the starch darkens her sleeves.
I dance under the dripping lines,
keeping time in the dark
of my closed eyes. I listen and move,
listen and move as the clothes
call me toward them. My mouth
leaves little half-moons where I kiss
the hems, my fingers make circles
on the waist of a dress.
I hug my arms across my chest and sway
back and forth to soothe an imaginary baby.

Upstairs at night my mother dreams, one hand
drawn into a fist. She is inventing
my life, the trees I will plant
outside the bathroom window, ruffles
with burns where the iron was too hot,
curtains that test the air as if they were wings
being tried for the first time.
She frets, "Heartaches," but feels the ache
low in the body. My unborn children turn
as she dreams of washtubs, the wringer waiting
while she carefully lifts her fingers
along the flute of a sleeve.

Photograph, 1952

The father springs from the 5:15 bus every night, happy
to be home, happy to eat his supper, to read his paper, to tell his girls
Mother knows best, happy to drink his ice water. (Gin.)
The smiling daughter shudders, puzzled,
recalling her mother's talk: *This is how it happens*,
her mother said, drawing a circle on a small square of paper
damp from the porcelain drainboard. *This is the egg*.
Then drawing a small dot, *This is the sperm* . . .
the sperm has to get inside the egg . . . The paper was thrown away.
They walked outside to have their picture taken.
The girl hides her confusion, her embarrassment.
In the photograph, the mother has a stunned look on her face,

as if seeing herself before the cry, before
the threatened blow.

She sleeps alone.
What will people think?
It is her fault. Of course.
It is all her fault.

Not My Life

I am the bitter goddess of less,
      scrunched and messy,
             moving backward
      in slow motion.

What I want has been torn
      off the page.
          I am fragments, edges,
      a waste of openings

gossiping to a mirror.
      I am a bowl
            filled with lemons,
      my favorite fruit.

Snowlight

My arms and legs sweep the snow in arcs.
An angel has fallen here
with a thud, embraced by gravity,
or, perhaps, she is what's left of me,
when, lips stiff, elbows locked,

I raise myself from the snow.
My mother's shadow erases the seamed and jagged

wings, snuffing out this epidemic
of lightheartedness.
As some sort of solution
I shout—Look! I'm hatching great angels!
My imagination sinks, as usual,

under the weight of my mother's sky.
I stamp the snow

where the angel in me burrows
with her awkward wings.
Watching from the house, my father

slowly dissolves in snowlight
until his image cannot be fixed in my mind.

The Dark Room

A little world, I spin
any way I can

past the shallow closet
with its clutch of striped ties
and open-toed high heels,
by the narrow bed
where the parents whisper
like statues come to life.

Caught in the gravity of their embrace,
I gaze into the frightening
depths of the ordinary

as if watching a ruined harbor
where the happiness of the world has sunk.

And I sink there knowing
I will be loved in this way:
the straight line of her mouth, his
rumpled hair, their marble skin
blurred by dark water.

What She Wants

a tree dropping persimmons
by a white wooden church
bees whispering

to bunched purple grapes
a train's deep breaths
slowing around a curve

a waiting girl striped
with sunlight, almost knowing
what she wants

Blackbird Poem

The world in the blackbird's song
repeating in my head,
it fills the senses
with the softness of not knowing.

Now a different key,
a virtuoso quaver at the end
the song proceeds, not probing
not an afterthought,
just here just here.

Cicadas

In my thirteenth year
that sound everywhere,
that shrillness night and day
as if it came from friction
between my cells. Which world
is this? I walk to school,
my dress still fresh
from the ironing—
rush of my skirts, empty husks underfoot—
the din insinuates, pulsates
with a terrible happiness.

The Conspirator

Meat sweating in the oven
while we sit through church.
Mother taps my knee and I steal
a sideways glance
as my father steadies the communion tray,
each glass of blood
oozing the body's original faults.

Thick, watery air under the lip of the rice pot,
earthy beets from little cans
at the bleached oak table. My mother
says, *That is the wrong fork, Let me pour the water.*
I hate the wallpaper, the antiqued bureau, the speckled plant.
A forkful held up, all at once, blood
and muscle, a body to bite into.

The membrane quivers, peas slide
off my plate as if the earth has tilted
because I, the conspirator,
have a secret so silent
it might be the voice of God.

Drought

An exploding bloom of sun
where the moon hung
last night. Still leaves above brown grass,
chicory static
along the edges, a froth
of pale underwater
plants on the surface.
The cold-blooded sun
compels me
to sacrifice flowers
for trees, new trees for old. Teasings
of rain, dark rumbles,
lightning—no lines
worth keeping.
Salt instead of sweat
between my breasts.

The Geometric Progression of Sadness

1

My grandfather wept and paced the floor
     for weeks after his wife and son
          died of influenza, leaving

him with two young daughters.
     He wanted to prepare them for life,
          what he called disappointment,

and had them dress for buggy rides,
     perch excitedly on the wooden seat,
          then said it was a lesson, go back inside.

2

For a Girl Scout badge I took a candid snapshot
of my mother on Saturday morning. She still
looks lost there in her dark
clothes, eyebrows not yet painted on.

She looked to me for the hard pebble
she wanted to find in her shoe.
Because she was afraid,
she could not bear my fears

and when I asked not to go to school,
she offered, in memory of her mother's death,
to send me away for good.

3

Invisible, my fingers brush the cheek
        of my older son. He rubs the spot,
                turning his intensity upon himself.

He does not remember the day his dog died,
        that because he did not cry I yelled at him,
                some senseless curse I'd heard

across the vast continent of childhood.

Stillbirth

The hopeless weight
turns cold, untouchable
yet I stay
with the dead child.
How can I leave?

My skin is stretched
out of love for you.
And what is love
but sacrifice,

the body
separating from grief.

The Persimmon Tree

Spots of dark bloom

ooze into melons. The persimmon
tree has grown into a frame. Still

the mother, still the child among the
branches. A gourd lies beside the spring

to satisfy thirst or purify the body, as if
there were a difference. Splatters shaken from a brush

break out along the stems of roses, soft
fists of buds safe inside the embroidery.

As the moon swells, the woman's hands ripen in the folds
of her gown. Under the tree, wells of shadows

swallow the persimmons as they fall, bleeding
the heart's juice into the shade.

Notebook: Allusion to Images

Words carved in stone erode.
The words are spaces
where gratitude has been chipped to sand.

Laid end to end words form a bridge, a wall,
a room. Edges of words snag on thoughts
like moored kites worrying in the wind.

The words are codes, camouflaged warriors
as dangerous as water: they expand and contract.
What if I told you one of the words is flint?

A single spark could ignite the page.

Blue Paper

The next time
I have something to say
I want bold
black capital
letters

set off
by blue paper
with faint embossed
designs

Oh look you will say
here are your words
and what is this
hidden beneath them

Recovering from Joy

The ocean, mindful of its rhythms,
inscribes hieroglyphics
of shells and charred wood across the sand.

I wade these shallows
watching for boats just back from deep water,
nets still wet on the deck
and the catch
gleaming with its ornament of bone,
almost recognizable.

Imagine the ritual,
the knotted ropes pulled tight,
the secret language of the crew,
and the bodies separating from grief.

Yet, how soon they drift,
clicking in figured boxes,
over the calm surface,
which reflects heat and light,
and the inverted images of happiness.

Song for Which There Are No Words

You come through the door with winter,
wind chimes fretting their same trail of notes.
Layers of sunset slant through the blinds

in the kitchen.
You trace the edge
of the table, I finger
the cloth. We reach across
what appears to be a limit.

It might as well be need, incurable,

dry pebbles under the tongue.
Love, love, the crickets' undersong
at intervals resuming.

I greet you, seeds in my hand,
waiting for rain.

A Scientific Education

Propped on the table,
your arm begins at the elbow,
fingers dangling carelessly
under your chin. I circle
your wrist with my fingers,

open the circle,
play my fingertips
down the warm slope,
memorizing the muscle's
round body. Then

I chart the edge of the bone
back up to your hand.
Following the natural order,
I smooth the fine hairs
that look black
in this light.

The Silent Ships

Sun from the east
heats the kitchen.
Snow, a bit of sky,
one swoop of hawk:
I rest in a patchwork of shadows.
This room has never
seen my past.
It is all future here.
As if I could levitate
out of my footsteps,
let go of myself
in Paris, hat falling
over my eyes,
olive beads lopsided
across my dress;
as if I could abandon
deserts or the Bosporus Strait
where I sipped lemonade
as ponderous ships
passed one another
like ghosts.

My Paradise Varies

1

Wind patterns the lake
like surfacing fish.

What can I wear
in the rain? All the clouds

in the sky.

2

Sunlight shreds the kitchen floor,
crusts of my mind

flaking, foreign again.
I think

in blue ink.

3

In snow, doves pepper
the trees like ornaments

What perfect
delight,

a clatter of joy.

4

I am writing food
instead of eating,

writing apples,
no more than

I can carry.

I Can Feel My Bones

I can feel my bones,
drier, finer-edged
than I remember.
My face, all angles,
wears a map
of simple lines.
Flat-spined,
my book of ribs
opens.

If Mykonos

If Mykonos

were mine
  the wind
        the bare

  hills
the startling
        light

the sea

                in far-flung
        blues and greens
could I
        could I

                give it away.

Red Curry

The waiter from Bangkok brings me fish and vegetables
       smothered in coriander and cayenne.
Beside the half-moon windows you feign polite
       interest over a cup of tea,
your free Saturday offered up to my passion
       for searing food. As you talk
of work and our children, I count off the links
       in my watch like the annular rings
of marriage. The blue wall behind you rises up
       like a great expanse of water your
wavering shadow adheres to, and I face two people,
       the transparent one overlapping
the man in the starched white shirt. My throat
       burns. "I can't describe it,"
I say, a forkful of fish, stained red,
       my message carrier.
I want to tell you about a dream
       where our silence
caused my fall from a cliff, how, refusing
       your help, I dug my fingers
into stone to bring myself back to you.
       What are we trapped in,
afraid to speak to one another? I swallow
       the fire in my mouth.
Carefully, we breathe the slow tides
       in and out, the once silver-
skinned fish between us reduced now
       to its narrow spine.

The Burning Woman

I am only valid when I burn,
the woman with flaming coils for hair.

Dressed in the finest, I like being noticed:
little pieces of anger secured with golden thread.

My encore will be armor.

There's such a buzzing inside my head
even my skull furrows. I sizzle

underwater. Little blisters
of air, my words rise

through wavy lines of heat.
I am weightless, inventing levitation.

Not Looking Back

a flight of stairs
in a different place
apples close to the water
I'm naked
laughing it off
flying very fast
the last party before waking
I forget about gravity
the trick
of returning

Carousel

One night, champagne-happy,
I threw my long-skirted leg
over the best white horse
on the carousel, laughing
as the Eiffel Tower moved
up and down around me.
When the calliope stopped,
I slid sideways off my sky-
high steed and three
women resting on a bench
nearby rose to catch me.
But, *voila!* I landed upright,
arms raised in a gymnast's V.
The women clapped.
Vendors were spinning
cotton candy, a vast
swath of filaments
dissolving to a spoonful.

Cold October Morning

(for Byron)

All excesses burned away, the trees
are reduced to their beginnings,
stenciled patterns
in the shape of open hands.

This is the seasonal unmasking
that comes to us, late,
after the eager green.
Now you walk slow steps
toward me. Your hands open

on my back, inside the shallow curve,
your bones aligning themselves.
I outline your thighs,
press to the underlying core.

Overhead winter birds circle the earth
as it turns toward the new moon,
which is invisible.

Revolutionary Music

Sleep-infected, my hand numb,
I write anything
I want as leaves of the silver

maple roll over
in the wind. All I have
are books, books everywhere,

that corridor of air
from centuries of breath.
I shuffle papers. My voice

harps like a beggar's
at a parade where torches
light the frozen river.

Lost

Nothing about this is easy.
       Maybe grief has to be learned a little each day.

           But of course, of course
               I don't know what I mean.

When I'm alone,
          I see someone just off to the right
      or left, not clearly, a slight figure about my height,
dark blue, no features, just a presence,
      a shape—

            startling—

        brief, not long enough
to know if I'm afraid.

      Without notes,
          without sketches,
              can I shift

out of perfect pitch
and drift
          toward the blue figure?

     That's asking a lot.

Deer on the Highway

In that moment of almost collision
when the deer looked at me
and we recognized one another,
I was unfamiliar but not trying to be
someone else who would lead me
away from myself.
I saw the deer's splendid eye,
the caramel-colored antlers.
Something forgotten, seen again,
the deer a monument
waiting to run.

Turning

I sleep girl-sleep,
the world

is whatever
I want it to be.

Outside, the moon
floats in the lake again

inside a rippling
necklace of rain.

I wake well-worn,
a goddess-woman

wearing the lake's
wrinkled skin.

The Sun

The sun is in place, always
the same place.

Sky pasted with clouds
lake studded with daylight.

The sudden swoop of herons
elongated, prehistoric.

Obedient as hibiscus
blooming for a day,

I open wide
my scarlet umbrella,

surrender to the sun
I encircle.

From the Bath

I settle my buoyant body in the depths,
gaze at the sky's colorless wash,
the tops of trees in the window,
leaves twisting over and under
like a Thai dancer's hands.
My cat's paws measure the air
as she sews herself to sleep.
A hawk croaks its clacking call.
I float to that first home,
all the world a private ocean, before the body's
cells left water for land.
In a smear of white a bird settles on the dead
branch of a tree, wings
arranging themselves
into clouds.

There will come a time
when I will forget my cat,
the hawk's prey
thumping my window,
when I will swim in a sea
with no horizons.

Swinging Statues

The edge of the world whirs by,
at first going one way, the trees,

another. The hand lets go
and we land unsteady on the ball

of a foot, a graceful arm
arced overhead, waiting

for the voice to shout *unfreeze*
but we can't hear,

such a roar from the questioning wind.
Was that it? We feel lopsided.

We want renewal,
another breath of ether.

We want another chance at the game.

This Poem Keeps Disappearing

I am writing myself into a hole
upside down half the time
my glasses are smudged

wasps flying off in all directions
I used to be strange in a perfectly normal way
but now I am older

this isn't fog, this is time
there's a hole in it
I need to find what it is and fill it

it doesn't take much, sleep
plucking loose ends
anchoring friends

this poem keeps disappearing
a scramble of silvery limbs
if only my fingers could do this without me

it is hard to write about a life I am still finding pieces for
the freedom from pretending
that joy

Child at the Edge of the World

A purple house, blue
sky on top, grass
electric green,

surrounded by the edge of the world
in a thick red line.
Rain smudges the clouds

and the girl on the crown
of the world's hill
as millions of eyes and ears

fall out of the sky
to look for the moon
and hear what I have to say.

Such Existence

A woman with such energy around her,
such existence,
that people move away
from that essence, dense and transparent,
when she enters a room.

She cannot confine herself to limits,
words on a postcard written around the address
and sideways in the margins,
what she says obliterated
by the postmark.

How has she settled into such existence,
seven decades of life
spilling over her like floating silk garments
in brilliant hues, in blacks, in colors so painful
they have no names?

All night the full moon blanket
drapes her chair where she wonders
why she has saved these layers
and who she would be without them.

Way In or Way Out

Trees in an evanescent dance.
Crows chasing the sun's
feverish profile.
A heron, the color of sky,
dissolving in the lake.

There then not there.
I'm someplace I've never been
as if my soul had separated

from the residue of who I used to be.
All year I watched the crows circling the woods.

On the Front Porch

The emphatic diagonals of herringbone
catch stray petals of dogwood

that I track into the kitchen,
where the soft gray of the cabinets
matches the early evening light.

Once, locked in winter
under hidden sparks of sun,

I navigated the world of books
and secrets packed down by numbness.

Now, spring is winning, as the sun
bursts into the kitchen and I am ready to bloom
or hatch or sing an aria.

The Apple

When the apple fell from the tree,
or did I fall from the tree,
the sun was ablaze with honeybees,
the lake blistered with blowing snow.

A nuthatch sliding upside down,
the sky was ground, the ground
was cloud, and all around me I forgot
and misery was my reverie. *Regret,*

yes, that old swamp,
regret and yet, for what—
let go let go the whirlpool said,
come back come back, pled

the passing flood and I was lost,
one foot in each. Rain will fall
some better place, some beach without
a roar, with a rock

to lay my head against,
a place I know no more.

The Road

There's this mean rock in my body
that my soul has to eddy around.

A rock of stubbornness, the rock
weighs me down,

anchors the trivia of my life.
All escapes are artificial

in artificial rain. There is no smell
of wet grass, of clean air,

no renegade heron I can almost
reach out and touch.

Light Years

I awake to snow
reflecting streetlamps,
once sharp-edged
grass now plump
with milkiness.
The telephone startles
as if energy from a planet
light-years away
suddenly reached
my bedroom, interrupting
my thoughts.
I answer before
my burgeoning cells
blur into
someone else.

The Moth

powdery wings fluster
around the light

a way of knowing
I want to borrow

that silver mystery
between worlds

my soul split at birth
and I have been wandering

with no cocoon

The End of My Life

1

Guilt is a box
of used bones.
I am who I am—
mossy, shining,
alive.

2

Before I am out of sight,
a statue sinking in a river,
set the table with a flowered cloth
and fresh strawberries.
I will wear red shoes
and bring a careful hunger.

3

I am still
but I am moving
aslant.
The earth absorbs my shadow.

4

The last particle of wind
disappears like a child
riding into the sea,
swallowed by something
nameless and complete.

Migration

The known world in flight,
the old horizon under our wings,
the sky clogged with leaves.

The light is alive,
the cataract of fog peeled away.
This opening, this reach.

Bright clouds underwater.
No secrets, no secrets.
The lake has no secrets.

Vibrating, beating,
substantial as bricks,
buoyant as breath, time is the sound we fall asleep to,
the thrum thrum of the washing machine,
the nonchalance of rain.

We thought we were mythologies,
hovering phantasms,
the consequence of wings.

Now everything makes sense.
I'm here, we say. I'm here too.
We pour out our lives like comets.

Night Journey

Stars frozen in grass,
moon deep
in ice,
lake swollen solid.

Inarticulate cold.
My bones jump.
What's beyond this startling weather?

Thoughts rub together
like flints.

I suppose
I can get there

without words.